Handbook for
HARD PLASTIC DOLLS
by Pam & Polly Judd

Published by Hobby House Press, Inc.
Grantsville, MD 21536

DEDICATION

To the After Dark Doll Study Club of Ohio. Members: John Axe, Dee Cermak, Barbara Comienski, Jim Comienski, Beverley Findlay, Pamela Judd, Shirley Karaba, Kathryn Koliha, Pat Parton, Deanna Pinizotto and Sandra Strater.

ACKNOWLEDGMENTS

Many thanks to the many people who have sent pictures of their hard plastic dolls. They are: Barbara Andresen, Vivien Brady, Barbara Comienski, Jean Francis, Marianne Gardner, Barbara Hill, Carol and Gerald Hiestand, Marge Meisinger, Peggy Millhouse, Elsie Ogden, Pat Parton, Rita Stice and Mary Ann Watkins.

Additional copies of this book may be purchased at $12.95 (plus postage & handling) from

HOBBY HOUSE PRESS, INC.

1 Corporate Drive
Grantsville, Maryland 21536

1-800-554-1447

or from your favorite bookstore or dealer.

Printed in the United States of America

ISBN: 0-87588-525-X

PREFACE

In the mid-1970s I began to collect dolls and was charmed by hard plastic dolls; however, like all new collectors, I needed to buy wisely and there was very little information available in published books. Since I was a researcher, I started to collect information and carried a pad of paper to write everything down. Suddenly I realized that I had enough information to write a book. My daughter Pam and I submitted it to Hobby House Press, and to our surprise and joy, they printed it. Our publisher is amazingly kind and so are the people who bought our books.

Throughout this book, I recommend repeatedly, ask questions of collectors and dealers. You will not only get information, you will gain many new friends.

Polly Judd

INTRODUCTION

Ten years after *Hard Plastic Dolls Volume I* was published, my husband Wally Judd asked to see the lockets he had made for me when he was a soldier during World War II. When he saw them, he said, "They are hard plastic! I made them from the new material which had been invented to fill the combat bullet holes and cracks in the airplanes during World War II." It had been his duty to teach the soldiers to repair disabled planes, and suddenly he had remembered the material they used. The new invention saved many lives and enabled many airplanes to get back into the air quickly. It also changed the manufacturing of many other products after the war.

Today only a few dolls are still made of hard plastic; however, many doll dealers tell us that the most asked for doll is a mint hard plastic one!

INVESTING IN DOLLS

Knowledge is important in investing. Throughout this book there will be tips about buying and selling dolls.

Beginning doll collectors should attend as many sales events as possible and ask dealers questions. These include doll shows, auctions, flea markets, garage sales, stores, television doll sales, advertisements in classified pages of newspapers and magazines, etc.

A & H Doll Corp.

Molly Pitcher, left and
Priscilla Alden, below.

Betsy Ross, left, and **Marie Antoinette,** right.

A & H Doll Corp.

Martha Washington, left, with a beauty spot on her chin, and **Mary Lincoln,** below.

Research Method

Doll collectors can contribute to their own sources of doll identification by searching out old advertisements, and by subscribing to doll periodicals and mail order catalogs.

Tell librarians about your wants and interests. They often base the purchases on periodicals and books on the needs of their clientele. Libraries also have sales of older books and magazines that are helpful for a home doll library.

Queen Victoria, left, and **Elizabeth I,** right.

Attending Auctions

1. Auctions are excellent places to research dolls and their prices even if you do not intend to buy anything. First send or call for a catalog.

2. Study the catalog carefully. Ask knowledgeable people for help before the auction.

3. Record auction prices in the catalog as the auction progresses.

4. Save and file catalogs.

5. You can also get the list of added dolls on the day of the auction, and write prices on it.

6. Early attendance will allow you to preview the dolls and record their condition. You cannot do this once the auction begins.

7. Be alert to the comments of other people previewing dolls, and jot them down also.

8. Auction aides will be there to answer questions.

9. Listen carefully to the auctioneer because he or she often gives helpful information, but train yourself to know when to stop bidding and not get caught up in "auction frenzy." At first, bid on inexpensive dolls. Set yourself a maximum bid and stick by it.

10. The auctioneer will state the rules of bidding. Listen carefully.

11. There are bargains at auctions. Gradually you will know them.

A & H Doll Corp.

Queen Isabella, left, and **Empress Eugenie,** right.

Conventions

Doll conventions are for fun, knowledge, and most of all for meeting doll friends from coast to coast. At various doll conventions, it is surprising to find such a variety of ideas, information and prices of dolls. UFDC (The United Federation of Doll Clubs, Inc.) hosts an annual convention. The fans of individual doll companies hold conventions. There are also local "gatherings." Most of them are advertised in doll publications. All these meetings usually end with the gift of a "souvenir doll."

Lady Elizabeth Grey (1461-1482), the young widow who married Edward IV. In this era, hats were often three feet tall. Street urchins mockingly called the cone-shaped hats a "steeple," but they were called a "hennin." The tiny black velvet loop on the forehead was only worn by women who had their own incomes of ten pounds a year, a magnificent amount on those days. The hats caused much difficulty for women, especially on the windy streets. Eventually they went out of style except in the classroom where they were called "dunce hats."

Alexander Doll Company

Fairy Queen, 18in (45cm) Margaret face; 1949-1950.
Marks: "ALEXANDER" on body. *Vivien Brady Collection.*

Kathy Ice Skater, an 18in (46cm) Maggie-face with pigtails, one of the early hard plastic dolls with a deeper facial color, circa 1949-1951.
Marianne Gardner Collection.

Knuckle-Head Nellie, inspired by Mary Martin's performance in the Broadway musical *South Pacific*. The doll is a painted hair, fully-jointed hard plastic of 14in (36cm). She has a reddish, short curly wig, a hair style introduced by Mary Martin, which created a new American trend. Marks: "Alexander" on back of neck.

Madame Alexander advertised for many years on the back cover of *Playthings Magazine*. This picture was on the May 1950 issue.

Godey Lady, 14in (36cm); early Margaret face. In 1950 and 1951 Alexander made elegant Godey dolls, both ladies and gentlemen. The card hanging from the doll's wrist is an auction number from a McMasters auction.

Louisa, 17in (43cm) painted hard plastic; fully-jointed; 1952.

In the early years of manufacturing, hard plastic dolls were painted. Chipping paint was a problem, so manufacturers quickly found a solution by adding color to the plastic material in the mold.

Jacqueline Kennedy, She is 21in (53cm), has vinyl arms, and wears a copy of Jacqueline Kennedy's historic satin ball gown; 1961-1962. **Marks:** "Mme Alexander" on back.

Alexander Doll Company

Gibson Girl, *Cissette* is 10in (25cm); 1963. **Marks:** "Mme Alexander" on back. *Marianne Gardner Collection.*

Wendy Ann Korea, *Maggie* mix-up face; 8in (20cm) bent knees; semi-rare; 1968-1970. *Marianne Gardner Collection.*

Alexander Doll Company

Queen Charlotte is a limited edition from the annual Alexander Convention, "Carolina On My Mind" of June 21-23, 1991. She is 9-1/2in (24cm); straight legs; sleep eyes. She is pictured with the related souvenirs that accompanied her. The carriage was the table centerpiece at the banquet. The English guard was also done for the Convention. MARKS on the tags on the costumes of these dolls: "MADC 1991. MADE IN U.S.A." Each doll's identification, "Queen Charlotte" and "English Guard," is also printed on the tag.

Searching for the Special Dolls

Begin by checking the advertisements in local newspapers for dolls for sale and for antique shows, garage sales, flea markets and doll shows. At shows record the dolls you like and their prices. Do not be afraid to ask the dealer for knowledge about the doll you are considering. If you are not satisfied with the price, ask if a lower price can be considered.

Many doll collectors prefer to look around the show before buying a doll; however, the doll may be gone when they return. That is why you should study the price guides so you will know a bargain when you see it.

Starting a doll collection is fun, but take time to ponder the prices of dolls you can afford. There are very nice inexpensive dolls as well as higher priced ones and expensive ones. There are ways to start a less expensive doll collection. If you are handy with cleaning, refinishing, sewing, etc., you can create a wonderful doll collection from less expensive or neglected dolls. My daughter Pam and I started this way, and we still cherish the ones we "fixed up."

Arriving in America from the **Wendy Ann Americana Collection of 1992.** 7-1/2in (19cm).

Other dolls from the *Americana Collection* are *Alaska, Graduation, Bobo the Clown, Betsy Ross, Majorette, Casey Jones, Scouting, Pocohantas, Holiday on Ice, Stilts, Little Devil, Witch, Bumble Bee, Cheerleader, Happy Birthday, Luck of the Irish, Ballerina, Flower Girl and Bride.*

Alexander Doll Company

Little Emperor, 8in (20cm): hard plastic: 400 made for the 1992 UFDC
Convention. **Marks:** "UFDC Luncheon//Little Emperor//by Madame
Alexander//Made in U.S.A."

Doll Auction Houses

Cobb's Auction Services
1909 Harrison Road
Johnstown, OH 43031

Frasher's Doll Auctions, Inc.
2323 S. Meclin School Road
Oak Grove, MO 64075

McMasters Worldwide
Productions
P.O. Box 1755
Cambridge, OH 43725

Theriault's
P.O. Box 151
Annapolis, MD 21404
Attn: Cynthia Gaskill

Convention Souvenir Books

A souvenir book from a UFDC National or Regional Convention is usually given to each person attending. It is full of different types of doll information. As the years pass these books are for sale in the secondary market or at auctions. They are excellent for a home library. For information about UFDC (the United Federation of Doll Clubs, Inc.) write: UFDC, 10920 North Ambassador Drive, Suite 130, Kansas City, Missouri 64153.

Sources of Information about Alexander Dolls

The Alexander Doll Company is still making and selling hard plastic dolls. There is also an active Alexander Doll Club. For information about membership write to Madame Alexander Doll Club, 298 Terrace Drive, Mudelein, Illinois 60060.

This book spotlights Alexander historical, literary and celebrity dolls. For further information consult the books *Hard Plastic Dolls Volumes I and II* by Polly and Pam Judd. They can be easily carried when you go shopping for dolls. To order these books and others call Hobby House Press at 1-800-554-1447.

Doll collecting will be a more enjoyable hobby if you have resources in your own home to identify and price your dolls.

Alexander & Aldon Industries

Alexander and Aldon Industries used the magic of Disney to make outstanding dolls in the 1950s. The Aldon company produced a special type of cutout plastic dolls to help children have a Magic Kingdom in their own home. In the late 1950s, Alexander made a *Cisette Tinker Bell* and a *Sleeping Beauty* doll with both a "Briar Rose" costume and a "Sleeping Beauty" long dress

Aldon Industries plastic cut-out **Tinker Bell** and Madame Alexander's **Cisette Tinkerbell,** 1950s.

Sleeping Beauty/Briar Rose cut-out plastic dolls by Aldon Industries and Madame Alexander's version, 1950s.

Walt Disney's Sleeping Beauty as a cut-out plastic set by Aldon Industries and a hard plastic doll by Madame Alexander, 1950s.

Allied Grand Doll Manufacturing Co., Inc.

This company made very early, small, inexpensive hard plastic play dolls which are similar to Knickerbocker, S & E and Reliable of Canada. (See *Hard Plastic Dolls Volume II,* pages 169, 214 and 223).

Shown are a child, baby and Indian: from *Playthings,* March 1949. **Marks:** "Allied Grand" on plastic heart-shaped tag.

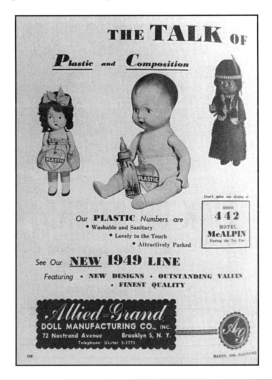

Research Tip

Playthings magazine is still a major publication of toy and doll manufacturers. Issues are sometimes available in antiques and collectibles or print shows. Local libraries can borrow copies of *Playthings* from regional libraries of the Library of Congress. The entire collection of *Playthings* is stored in the John Adams Building of the Library of Congress in Washington, D.C. For doll collectors this is one of the best doll resources available and well worth a trip to Washington.

American Character Doll Company

Sweet Sue in original box: 14in (36cm); hard plastic head attached to walking mechanism; saran hair; nylon dress trimmed with lace and flowers; matching socks and shoes; straw bonnet; advertising brochure of *Baby Toddles* in box; 1950s. *Courtesy McMasters Worldwide Productions.* **Marks:** "Sweet Sue, Queen of Dolls" on wrist tag; "1015" label on box.

Sweet Sue comes in various sizes. For further information see *Hard Plastic Dolls Volume I* pp. 43-50 and *Hard Plastic Dolls Volume II* pp. 43-48.

This *Sweet Sue* is an example of the type of doll called "mint-in-box" that most collectors seek diligently. Even the pamphlet advertising other American Character dolls is still in the original box.

American Character Doll Company

Betsy McCall: 8in (20cm); bisque-like finish; rooted hair in plastic skull cap; blue, sleep eyes with molded lashes; closed mouth; knee joints; 1958. Additional clothes could be purchased; commercial patterns for dolls were available. *Sandra Strater Collection.* **Marks:** "McCall Corporation" on back of doll.

Note: Old *McCalls* magazines with paper dolls can sometimes be purchased at doll and paper collectible shows.

Ardee Company

Fashions for Dolls. Children always liked to change costumes on dolls. Some manufacturers, such as Alexander, made extra clothes for their dolls. Additional clothes from doll fashion houses, such as Ardee, were also sold. Although some collectors insist the doll must have the original outfits, others want both types. Collectors also enjoy sewing reproduction costumes from the old patterns that are often available at doll shows or by advertising in doll periodicals. Shown are Ardee doll fashions from *Playthings,* March 1953.

Arranbee Doll Company

An advertisement for **Nanette.** *Playthings,* October 1950. The dolls are 15in (38cm), 18in (46cm) and 23in (58cm). They have dynel or saran wigs, personal combs, and instruction sheets. Dolls, left to right are: *Nanette* "Tea Party," *Nanette* "Roller Skater" and *Nanette* "Party Formal."

Arranbee Doll Company

Littlest Angel Bride: 11in (28cm); head-turning walker; jointed knees; sleep eyes; stiff net bridal dress with lace trim; pearl heart at neckline; flowers in hair; veil is missing; pictured in 1957 brochure. **Marks:** "R & B" on head.

Littlest Angel: 9in (25cm); pin-jointed, head-turning walker; sleep eyes; molded eyelashes; dimples on back of hand; rooted hair; molded tongue. She wears a jodhpur costume from 1955-1957.

For more information see: *Hard Plastic Dolls Volume I,* pp. 51-55 and *Hard Plastic Dolls Volume II,* pp. 50-62, including Angel catalog. **Marks:** "R & B" on back of neck.

Cosmopolitan

The Cosmopolitan company made *Ginger* wardrobe dolls that competed with the Vogue's *Ginny* and Alexander's *Wendy-Kin.* They were less expensive, but colorful and durable. The ones dressed in the Disney's Mouseketeer costumes bring high prices. The "Mickey Mouse Club" television show of 1955-1959 was very popular. Children could become "mouseketeers" and receive hats with Mickey Mouse ears.

The 7-1/2in (18cm) **Ginger** dolls wear official costumes worn by cast members including large ears and Mickey Mouse masks. The Hungerford Plastic Corporation obtained a Disney license to produce the dolls. See *Hard Plastic Dolls Volume I,* pp. 81-82 and *Hard Plastic Dolls Volume II,* pp. 78-85 for more information and identification tips.

Artisan Novelty Company of California

Television was new and exciting in 1951 when it launched the 20in (51cm) **Raving Beauty** dolls with a unique, very wide walking mechanism. Today they are called fashion dolls and collectors eagerly search for these dolls with different clothing and hair styles. The dolls shown are from the *Ima Moreland Collection*. See *Hard Plastic Dolls Volume I*, pp. 56-57 and *Hard Plastic Dolls Volume II*, pp. 63-66 for more pictures and information. *Marks:* None on doll. Tags on some clothing.

Miss Moppet with wardrobe, Marshall Field 1954 catalog.

Miss Moppet walks when you lead her, moves her head. Saran pigtails can be combed, rebraided; thickly lashed eyes close. She's ready for anything with a cotton dress, bonnet, socks, shoes, purse. Wardrobe holds tartan dress, panty, jacket, bonnet, checked dress, straw hat, cotton felt coat 'n' hat, robe, nightgown, slippers, skates, shoes, purse, curlers. 11 inches tall, plastic. Ages 5 to 10.
151 T2-92 . . . .**$9.95**

Doll to play with and love

Junior Miss with a complete wardrobe. She's off to school in wool skirt, broadcloth blouse, hand knit sweater, 2-tone sport shoes . . . she even totes a notebook and pencil in her book strap! 18-inch metal trunk holds: frothy formal, cotton felt coat 'n' hat, school dress, short party dress, beruffled half slip, garter belt, bra, nightgown, towel, washcloth, fan, beads, socks, bead evening bag and her first long nylons. Also has two pairs of shoes, skates, sun glasses, slippers, straw hat. 18 inches tall, fully jointed, all plastic, nylon wig. Ages 6 to 12. **151 T7-7** $49.95

We're sorry . . . but we cannot promise delivery before Christmas on orders received after December 18.

Junior Miss with wardrobe and trunk, Marshall Field 1955 catalog.

Research Tools for Identifying Dolls

1. Collect new and old doll books, price guides and old doll catalogues to help you identify old dolls.

2. Subscribe to one or more of the doll magazines or newsletters. Write to the editor suggesting they have articles about the dolls that interest you.

3. Join by-mail doll clubs, such as *Alexander* and *Barbie,* who issue newsletters regularly.

4. An excellent program for a doll club is sharing books, catalogs and other information used for identifying dolls.

Spiegel Catalog Dolls of the 1950s: Baby dolls and young child dolls occupy the top section. They all had crying voices. The bottom section has a girl skater doll and brides and bridesmaids dolls, which were popular in the period after World War II. *Barbara Andersen Collection.*

Chiquita Doll

Orange Queen: 7-1/2in (19cm); blonde hair; jointed at neck and shoulders; movable eyes.

Chiquita made inexpensive costume dolls. The line included: 1. *Lupe, Mexican Hat Dancer* 2. *Miranda, Cuban Congo Dancer* 3. *Carmina, Castillian Lady* 4. *Fluffy Duff, First Date* 5. *Nilda Central American Costume* 6. *Marquese, Queen's Lady in Waiting* 7. *Bimini Woman, Caribbean Island Costume* 8. *Tropicana, Island Market Doll* 9. *Carlotta with Baby.*

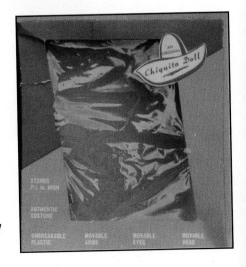

Duchess Doll Corporation

Gibson Girl: sleep eyes; fully-jointed; 1948-1950s. *Carol Hiestand Collection. Photograph by Gerald Hiestand.* **Marks:** "Duchess Doll Corp. Design Copyright 1948."

Many collectors have enjoyed starting their hobby with inexpensive, but beautiful hard plastic dolls. If glamorous adult dolls are important to you, *Duchess* dolls, which often come with original clothes in the original box, are a good way to start a collection and an easy way to store it.

Duchess Doll Corporation

Mideastern Costume Doll: 8in (20cm). *Duchess* dolls were made between 1948 and the 1960s. *Carol Hiestand Collection. Photograph by Gerald Hiestand.* For more information see *Hard Plastic Dolls Volume I* pp. 85-86 and *Hard Plastic Dolls Volume II* pp. 99-102. **Marks:** "Duchess Doll Corp. Design Copyright 1948."

Effanbee

Playmate: 26in (66cm). She sings "London Bridge," recites "Mary had a Little Lamb," says "Mama" and "Daddy," laughs gleefully, and prays "Now I lay me down to sleep." This doll, called "Playmate" in a 1950s Spiegal catalog, is *Sweetie Pie.* She has a hard plastic head, a cloth body and vinylite plastic limbs. Extra clothing and bedding were also available for the doll.

Junior Miss Ballerina: hard plastic body; vinyl head and arms; 18in (46cm); 1958. *Barbara Comienski Collection.* **Marks:** "Effanbee" on head.

In 1949 Effanbee introduced its first hard plastic dolls. They were *Honey* and two baby dolls. The buyer had a variety of clothes from which to choose. This advertisement from *Playthings,* July 1945 shows: **Momma's Baby** with hard plastic painted head with sleep eyes with lashes and a latex body stuffed with cotton. **Dy-Dee Baby.** She still had a composition head, a rubber body and applied rubber ears. *Dy-Dee* could drink from a bottle and wet her diaper. By 1950 the doll had a hard plastic head. **Honey** was Effanbee's first hard plastic girl doll.

Tintair: 16in (41cm); sleep eyes; long blonde hair; mint in box. For a color picture and explanation of the hair tint, see *Hard Plastic Dolls Volume II* p. 163. *Pat Parton Collection.*

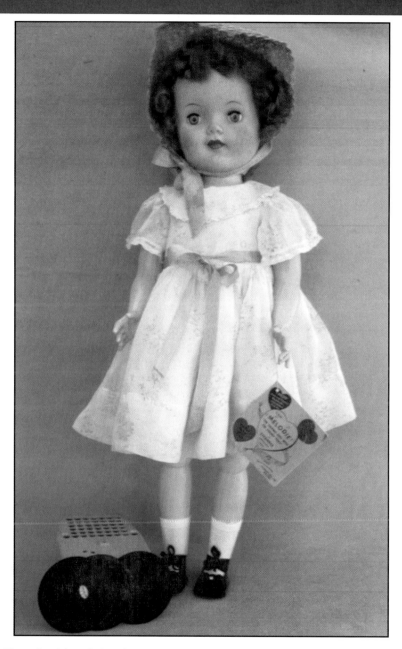

Melodie: vinyl head; hard plastic body, 27in (69cm); jointed knees; walking, talking, singing, kneeling, praying; uses flashlight batteries; original except shoes and socks; 1953-1956. *Barbara Comienski Collection.* **Marks:** "Effanbee" on head.

G.H. & E. Freydberg, Inc.

Mary Jane: This *Terri Lee* look-alike was advertised as "the doll who has and does Everything [sic]." She was less costly than a *Terri Lee* doll. 17in (43cm); fully-jointed; choice of hair styles and colors; flirty eyes; nice wardrobe available but lacking *Terri Lee's* quality. 1955. **Marks:** "Mary Jane" sewn on tag on clothing. For more information see: *Hard Plastic Dolls Volume I* p. 113 and *Hard Plastic Dolls Volume II* p. 104.

Hausser-Elastolin (Germany)

Bild Lilli: 11-1/2in (31cm); European-type hard plastic with celluloid base. She is a "curvey" high-heeled fashion-type doll with pony tail and "spit" curl; body parts are connected with a large elastic band. There is also a 7-1/2in (19cm) version of this doll. *Aurelina Rodriguez Collection.*

The inspiration of this popular German doll came from a cartoon character *Lilli,* drawn by Rheinard Beuthien for the German newspaper *Bild-Zettung. Lilli* was very popular in European countries, and a few dolls were imported into the United States. The doll pictured was purchased with another doll at a street fair in Greece for 500 drachmas (about $1.80 for both dolls). The sports clothes are original.

Mattel discovered the dolls in Europe. Since dolls with wardrobes were already important in the United States, the company decided the "curvy" figure might be popular. This was the inspiration for *Barbie®. Aurelina Rodriguez Collection.*

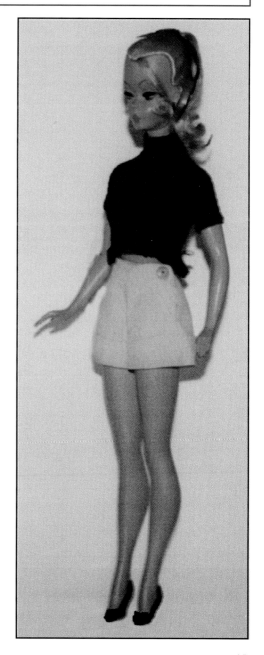

Hasbro, Inc., (Hassenfeld Bros.)

Little Miss Seamstress set features a Necchi sewing machine molded in plastic. Made in U.S.A. 11in (28cm). There is a needle, thread, ribbons, lace, and material enough to make a party dress, sport dress and house dress. 1950s. *Pat Parton Collection.* **Marks:** "Hasbro // U.S.A." on dolls.

Horsman

Christmas Dolls from a Spiegel Catalog of the 1950s. Row 1: Babies and toddlers: *Twinkles, Lambie, Candy, Linda, Honey Lou* and *Baby Sue.* Row 2: All hard plastic: *cowboy, cowgirl, nun,* two *bridesmaids, bride and groom.* Row 3: *baby girl with real hair* and *curlers* and *big cuddle dolls.*

Ideal Toy Corporation

(and Dorothy Creations, Inc.)

Doll manufacturers have always tried to imitate best-selling dolls. This was especially true during the hard plastic era. All three dolls pictured have the same style and color dresses and similar hair. This particular group of dolls is unusual and rare. They were for sale and displayed together at a doll show in Chicago.

In the center is a **Dorothy Creations** doll in her original box. She is 16in (41cm); saran hair; complete with play wave kit. *Marks:* "Dorothy Creations Inc." At the left is Ideal **Toni**: P-91, 16in (41cm); at the right a 21in (53cm) **Toni**. All three dolls have similar style and color dresses and similar hair. *Vivien Brady Collection.*

Many baby dolls were made of hard plastic by most of the American doll companies. Ideal made many excellent ones; however, if they were not properly cared for the hard plastic would break, and many of them did not survive.

Large Ideal Baby: Hard plastic head; legs and arms; cloth body; open mouth with teeth; sleep eyes; molded hair with curl in middle of forehead; all-original. *Marianne Gardner Collection.* **Marks:** "P 50//Ideal Pat Pending."

Advertisement for *Betsy McCall* and *Mary Hartline* dolls in *Playthings* magazine, March 1953. Both dolls use the *Toni* body; *Mary Hartline* also uses the *Toni* head.

Betsy McCall (on left): 14in (36cm); vinyl head; hard plastic body. *Mark:* "McCALL CORP" on head; "P-90 IDEAL" on back. **Mary Hartline** (on right), represents the band leader from television's "Super Circus." She came with a majorette's baton. **Mark:** "IDEAL DOLL MADE IN U.S.A." on head; "IDEAL DOLL P-91" on body.

Betsy McCall: 14in (36cm); hard plastic body; vinyl head; brown sleep eyes; 1953. *Sandy Strater Collection.*

During this time period, *McCall's* published a Betsy McCall paper doll with the latest fashions for little girls each month. **Marks:** "Official Betsy McCall Doll//Copyright 1952" on tag. "Ideal Corporation" on doll.

Mary Hartline by Ideal. 1952-1953. 22-1/2in (57cm). All-original with original baton and hang tag. **Mark:** "IDEAL DOLL // P-94" on back. *John Axe Collection.*

Howdy Doody, circa 1953. He is 25in (64cm), has a jointed ventriloquist mouth on a hard plastic head, a cloth body with vinyl hands and is all-original. **Mark:** "IDEAL DOLL" on the head. *John Axe Collection.*

Howdy Doody, circa 1953. 20in (51cm) and 25in (64cm). Hard plastic heads with a ventriloquist mouth; cloth bodies; vinyl hands. They are all-original. **Mark:** "IDEAL DOLL" on heads. *John Axe Collection.*

Lenci

After World War II the Lenci company of Torino, Italy, experimented with new, smaller souvenir-type dolls. Lenci, and other European doll and toy companies, developed a compound similar to hard plastic but it was based on celluloid. It was safer and sturdier than the flammable and fragile celluloid used previously. Lenci continued to dress the dolls with the company's own style of excellent clothing.

Avigliano // Lucania Regional Girl. 8in (20cm); jointed arms only; painted face. **Marks:** "Lenci//Torino//Made in Italy," on a round silver paper tag; "30 Avigliano" on second tag.

Calabria, Torino and **Venezia Tridentina,** left to right. Lenci dolls from the 1950s to 1970s: 6in (15cm); solid, celluloid-based compound Lenci bodies; painted faces; unusual eyebrows; jointed arms; painted shoes; dressed in provincial clothes.**Marks:** All three dolls: "Lenci Torino" on cloth tag sewn into costume.

Lenci

Carabiniere (Policeman) and **Milano:** 9in (23cm) each; European-type hard plastic with celluloid base. **Marks:** The Certificato of Origine has "Lenci" on the inside. The lady also has a "Lenci, Torino" tag sewn in the skirt.

Sardegna (Sardinia): 11in (28cm); European celluloid-based hard plastic which feels like hard felt. **Marks:** "SARDEGNA" on celluloid type of tag with hand-painted flowers which can be seen doubled-over near waist in picture.

H.D. Lee Co., Inc.

Buddy Lee: 12in (31cm); denim engineer costume; gold buttons with *Lee* on them; about 1950.

Marcie
(A Marketing Company of A & H Doll Co.

In 1952 A & H created the new *Marcie Doll line*. The dolls were advertised in the July, 1952, issue of *Playthings*. Soon a similar doll, *Donna, Marcie's* quick-selling sister, was produced. They are both 12in (31cm). Other A & H dolls included *Gigi, Birthstone Dolls* and *Quick-selling Sister.*

Marcie

In the hard plastic period, there were only a few companies manufacturing basic hard plastic dolls. Some only made undressed dolls. Others added hair, clothing, etc. and marketed the dolls themselves. Marketing companies would buy dolls, dress them, and sell them.

Individual doll designers would purchase dolls and design clothing lines for sale to department stores and individuals (see *Mollye.*) The larger marketing companies sold similar lines of dolls. **Ken Murray's Glamour Cowboys** is an example of several differences between two dolls which look alike. The doll on the left is smaller and a cheaper grade of hard plastic. Since the costumes look the same, Marcia may have ordered bodies from two different companies or copied another company. Doll collectors need to consider these variations when identifying dolls and adding them to a collection.

Molly'es Fashions
for Hard Plastic Dolls

Molly Goldman was famous for her costuming of dolls. She worked for many different companies including Horsman, Effanbee and Ideal. The best known doll costumes she designed were for the *Shirley Temple* doll in the 1930s. She also designed clothes for unmarked hard plastic dolls which were marketed with only a tag on the dress. Some of her clothing was sold separately in select stores. *Rita J. Stice Collection.* **Marks:** "MOLLYE" on dress tag. None on doll.

Nancy Ann

Muffie: 8in (20cm); saran or dynel wigs; individual fingers; closed mouth; all have similar bodies with minor differences; circa 1953-1956. Dolls at left to below: three straight leg walkers and two head-turning walkers. *Mary Ann Watkins Collection.* For more information see *Hard Plastic Volume I* p. 190 and *Hard Plastic Dolls Volume II* pp. 151-155. **Marks:** "STORY BOOK// DOLLS//CALIFORNIA" on backs.

Lori-Ann Girl and Boy: 8in (20cm); turning head, straight-leg walker; sleep eyes; rosier skin than *Muffie;* red haired girl; flocked, brown-haired boy. *Special Clue to Identification of Girl:* She has a row of reddish curls on the back of head. *Muffie* has a different hair style. Both are *very rare* dolls. **Marks:** None on dolls, but name is on polka dot box.

Niresk Industries, Inc.

Niresk was a major catalog company in the 1950s. First Row: **Sweet Sue** *by* American Character: 31in (69cm); vinyl head; rooted hair; hard plastic body; head-turning walker; knee, hip, elbow, shoulder joints; kneels for prayers; sleeps. All American Girl*:* 25in (64cm) walker; vinyl head; rooted hair; hard plastic body; leather-like jacket and cap, pleated skirt. **Angel Face:** 23in (58cm); vinyl head with rooted pony tail; hard plastic body; jumper-type dress; sits, sleeps, head-turning walker. Second Row: **Rita** from Paris Doll Company; 30in (76cm) hard plastic; head-turning walker; pony tail; stands, sits alone; plaid dress. **Ritzy Fritzy***:* head-turning walker; hard plastic; print dress; fur coat, hat, muff, hair. **Miss Dimples***:* 29in (74cm); head-turning walker; sleep eyes; glazed cotton dress; organdy apron.

Catalog 1955

First Row: Four dolls (left hand side): 20in (51cm); dolls have vinyl heads with saran hair; walking dolls; sit, stand, cry, turn heads. **Lassie Braids:** Girl in plaid dress; blonde pigtails. **Lana Longbob:** Girl with brown short hair; blue top, white print skirt. **Shirley Short Bob:** Newest Italian movie star hair cut. **Penny Ponytail:** Glamorous party-goer in glazed cotton, lace-trimmed pinafore.

First Row fifth doll: **Dorothy Collins** (singer on "Your Hit Parade" on TV): sizes 14in (36cm), 18in (46cm), 23in (56cm). First Row sixth doll: **Alice Walks out of Wonderland:** 15in (41cm) and 21in (53cm); hard plastic; blonde long hair; head-turning walker. Bottom Row: **Janie Pigtail, Baby Trix, Winnie, Posie**.

Niresk Indusctries, Inc.

Nina Ballerina: 20in (51cm); vinyl head; rooted saran hair; hard plastic body; kicks and splits as head turns from side to side; wears ballet tutu.

Dream Princess: 22in (56cm); vinyl head; saran hair; hard plastic body; walking mechanism; hold hands and she walks; nylon gown with tulle trimmed with silver sequins and flowers.

Cinema Bride: 21in (53cm); hard plastic; walking mechanism; shimmering bridal gown and veil; beribboned bouquet.

Belle of the Ball: 26in (66cm); vinyl head with saran hair; hard plastic body; sits, sleeps, cries.

Patty Ponytail: 25in (26cm); vinyl head; saran rooted hair; hard plastic body; sits, sleeps, cries.

Play Doll with Cotton Dress: walking doll; vinyl shoes and bobby socks.

Pedigree
(of England)

Princess Ann as Small Child: 14in (36cm); hard plastic; fully jointed; sleep eyes; blonde mohair wig; red, dotted Swiss dress with red trim; 1953.

Princess Ann as a Toddler was pictured on the cover of *Woman's Illustrated,* a very popular woman's magazine in England. For more information, see *Hard Plastic Dolls Volume II* pp. 183-184. **Marks:** "PEDIGREE" on back of neck.

Plastic Molded Arts

Seminole: 15in (38cm); hard plastic; head-turning walker; sleep eyes; open mouth; two teeth; black mohair wig; 1949-1955. *Marks:* "Plastic Molded Arts//L.I.C. New York".

Plastic Molded Arts made various grades of dolls and parts for many other companies. For more information about this prolific company, see *Hard Plastic Dolls Volume I* pp. 207-211.

Reliable of Canada

Established in 1920 in Toronto, Ontario, the Reliable Toy Co. has a long tradition of making fine dolls. Although they introduced their own line of dolls, the Reliable Company did buy molds from American companies, especially the Ideal Toy Corporation.

Queen Elizabeth II Coronation Doll: All hard plastic in regalia robes; 1956. This was given away as a premium by the Dominion stores of Canada. *Jean Francis Collection.*

Richwood Toys, Inc.

Richwood Toys, Inc. made its **Sandra Sue** dolls in Annapolis, Maryland, and sold them primarily on the east coast of the United States. The company made limited editions of the *Sandra Sue* dolls for special occasions. This doll is called *Sophie Smith.* She was made for a 45th class reunion of Smith College. A special party was hosted by Edith Scott at her summer home in Westhampton in honor of Susan Smith of the class of 1909. Each visitor was given a *Sandra Sue* doll specially dressed in a white rayon dress with a yellow banner that says, "1909-1954." Her special wig was dark brown with blue flowers in it. This is one of the rarest *Sandra Sue* dolls. *Sandra Strater Collection.*

Sandra Sue: 7-1/2in (19cm); sleep eyes; flat feet; blonde wig with double stitched part. *Peggy Millhouse Collection. Photographs by Peggy Millhouse.* **Marks:** None on dolls.

Richwood Toys, Inc.

Sandra Sue: Clothing is by Mrs. Ida Wood, doll artist and owner of Richwood Toys. Wigs have side parts with double stitching. *Peggy Millhouse Collection. Photograph by Peggy Millhouse.*

Sandra Sue in Formal Attire: Richwood featured slender, movable figures for stylish clothes. It was ball-jointed so it could sit, stand, walk and move her head and arms. The beautiful face was possibly created by sculptor Agop Agopoff. *Peggy Millhouse Collection. Photograph by Peggy Millhouse.*

Richwood Toys, Inc.

Sandra Sue Dolls on See Saw: Two dolls wearing schoolgirls pleated skirt and blazer with tam. *Barbara Hill Collection.* **Marks:** "Sandra Sue See Saw-300" printed on base.

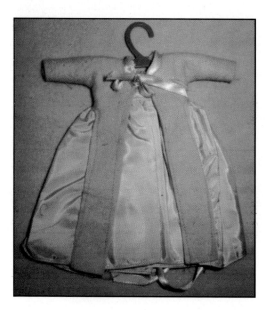

Negligee for Sandra Sue: Clothes were sold separately and could be ordered by mail. They came on a special hanger and plastic cover. *Elsie Ogden Collection.*

Sandra Sue dolls with a grown-up appearance. Note the more mature clothing, the high-heeled shoes and the shapely legs. *Peggy Millhouse Collection. Photograph by Peggy Millhouse.*

Cindy Lou: 14in (36cm); head-turning walker; pin-jointed knees; hair in pigtails; clothes advertised as "Round the Clock Fashions." *Barbara Hill Collection.*

Cindy Lou: She was one of the line of dolls made by the company which marketed the well-made furniture for the dolls. 14in (36cm); walking, head-turning; pin jointed knees. Their line of clothing was called "Round the Clock Fashions." *Barbara Hill Collection.* **Marks:** "MADE IN U.S.A." in circle on back. For more information see *Hard Plastic Dolls Volume II* pp. 190-196.

Richwood Toys, Inc.

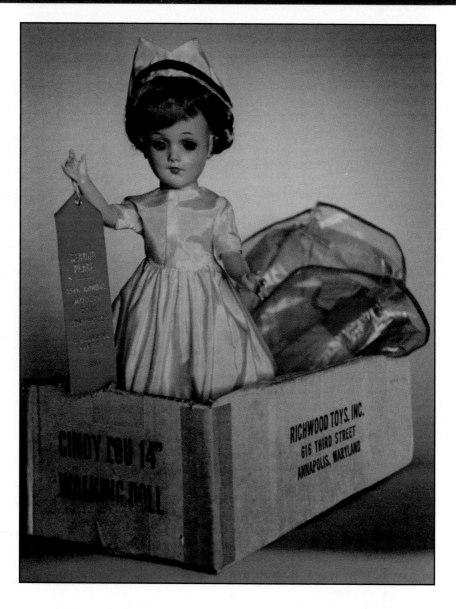

Cindy Lou: 14in (36cm); hard plastic; nurse in shipping box; pink plastic in back of box is a dust cover for *Cindy Lou* clothes. *Peggy Millhouse Collection. Photograph by Peggy Millhouse.* **Marks:** "CINDY LOU" on box.

Collectors of Richwood dolls are fortunate to have beautiful well-made furniture such as the clothes hanger and a mahogany bed along with a complete set of bedding to seek as well as the dolls. *Barbara Hill Collection. Photograph by Barbara Hill.* **Marks:** "Made in USA" (in circle on back).

Cindy Lou and Sandra Sue Getting Ready for Bed: Matching pink satin gowns. *Barbara Hill Collection. Photograph by Barbara Hill.* For more information about Richwood Toys, see *Hard Plastic Dolls Volume II* pp. 190-197.

Roberta Doll Co., Inc.

Roberta Ann Bride: 14in (36cm); hard plastic; golden hair that can be washed, combed, curled, waved and set; plastic rollers; sleep eyes; open mouth with teeth; dressed in flocked organdy and lace bridal clothes with net veil; mid-1950s. **Marks:** "Made in U.S.A.//Patent Pending" on back of neck.

Roberta Doll Company & Cast Distributing Corp.

Holeloke with Hawaiian Wardrobe in Trunk: 18in (46cm); open mouth with teeth; red felt tongue; walking doll; green print two-piece shorts and bra set; multicolored skirt and sarong top; 1950s. *Kathy Kolina Collection.* **Marks:** "Made in U.S.A." on back of doll.

Rønnaug Petterssen
(of Norway)

Hardanger (Province) Bride and Groom. The groom is 18in (46cm); the bride is 19in (48cm). The European hard plastic bodies are a compond made from a celluloid base. They are from the 1960s. *Sandra Strater Collection.* **Marks:** "Hardanger (Province)" and two Rønnaug Petterssen seals on box.

Rosebud

Miss Rosebud: 7in (18cm). In 1947 Eric Smith of Raunds, Northampton, registered a trademark for "Rosebud" dolls in imitation of the Ginny-type dolls in the United States. The walking doll pictured is dressed to match the name. There is a variety of costumes for this doll. In 1967 Mattel took over the company. *Marge Meisinger Collection.* **Marks:** "Miss Rosebud" on head; "Rosebud" on body.

English Coronation Peeress: 16in (41cm); full-jointed; sleep eyes; open mouth with two teeth; beautiful reddish-brown mohair wig; buxom breasts added with padding. **Marks:** "Rosebud//Made in England//PAT. NO 667906" on back; "Rosebud" on head.

Star Doll Company

Dorothy Collins: 14in (36cm); walking doll; gold saran hair; several larger sizes; mid 1950s. **Marks:** "MADE IN U.S.A." on back. "Dorothy Collins Doll" on tag.

Terri Lee

Advertisement for Terri Lee Family of dolls by Vi Gradwohl of Apple Valley, California, in *Playthings,* March 1955. Shown are *Terri Lee, Jerri Lee, Bonnie Lou* and *Baby Linda.*

Terri Lee Cowgirl: Late 1940s, early 1950s. 16in (41cm); all-original. This is the original, shiny hard plastic used by Terri Lee; the later dolls had a more traditional hard plastic formula. **Marks:** "Terri Lee, Pat. Pending."

Togs and Dolls Corp.

Mary Jane: 17in (43cm); hard plastic body; unusually large vinyl head; sleep eyes with lashes; golden brown hair; fully jointed; head-turning walker; dimples below fingers and on knees; unusual arm hook. See *Hard Plastic Dolls Volume I* p. 267. **Marks:** None on doll; "My name is Mary Jane; I am made of Celanese acetate plastic; I have 36 pretty outfits. Do you have them all?" on tag.

Unknown

Nancy and Slugo: These dolls are rare and have been reported to have been made in England. They also have characteristics of Reliable of Canada, Virga, Fortune, and other American companies. They have a lighter weight hard plastic than most American dolls. Both dolls are 7-1/2in (19cm); full-jointed. *Sandra Strater Collection.*

Virga

Mary, Mary, Quite Contrary How does your Garden Grow? Good quality, shiny hard plastic from the *Nursery Rhyme Series;* fully-jointed. Virga dolls are usually colorful, entertaining and inexpensive. They competed with the Vogue *Ginny* dolls. Often these dolls can still be found in pristine condition like this one.

Vogue

Jenny Graves founded the Vogue doll company in the 1930s and experimented with various doll-making materials. Her first choice was composition, for the doll called *Toddles*. She changed to hard plastic in 1948.

Ginny Ice Skater from the "Sports Series," 1952. 8in (20cm); sleep eyes with painted lashes above eyes; straight legs. *Marianne Gardner Collection.* **Marks:** "Vogue" on head and body.

Ginny Walker: sleep eyes; painted lashes; black vinyl shoes marked "Ginny" on heel. The tag on the right side is her auction tag. *Courtesy McMasters Worldwide Productions.* **Marks:** "Ginny" and "Vogue Dolls, Inc. Made in U.S.A."

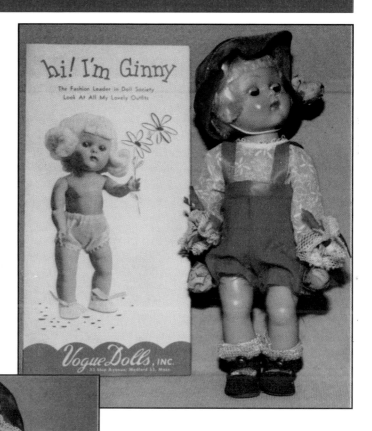

Hansel and Gretel from the "Twin Series," 1950-1953. 8in (20cm); fully-jointed; sleep eyes; painted lashes; matching pink and white costumes. *Sandra Strater Collection.* **Marks:** None.

Ginny Skier, circa 1955. 8in (20cm); sleep eyes with molded lashes; red hair. For more information about Vogue dolls see *Hard Plastic Dolls Volume I* pp. 245-257 and *Hard Plastic Dolls Volume II* pp. 214-228.

INDEX

INDEX